TRANSFORM FROM AN **EMPLOYEE MINDSET**

ENTREPRENEUR SUCCESS MANUAL

CATRINA L. WILLIAMS

Table of Contents

Preface

Quick Success Tips

Chapter 1. Introduction to Entrepreneurship

Chapter 2. Self-Assessments

Chapter 3. Brainstorm

Chapter 4. Planning Phase

Chapter 5. Research & Notate

Chapter 6. Financial Management

Chapter 7. Business Plan

Chapter 8. Marketing Plan

Chapter 9. Business Resources

Chapter 10. Action Steps

All Rights Reserved. (C) 2017 by Catrina Latrice Williams-Hoolasie

Charleston, SC

No part of this book may be reproduced or transmitted in any form or by any means, electronic, or mechanical, including photocopying, recording, or by any information storage and retrieval system, without permission in writing from Catrina L. Williams-Hoolasie.

Created in the United States of America

Quick Success Tips

Read daily & Apply

* Develop an Open Mind and Keep It Motivated

* Willing to listen to a new mentor who have what you desire

* Willing to think outside what your peers would tell you not to do

* Willing to try new things outside your comfort zone

* Willing to ask questions when you do not understand

* Willing to take risks during your fearful moments

* Apply Organization Skills

* Time Management

* Money Management

* Always take written notes

* Pray for Patience

* Listen actively

* Pray consistently

* Don't give up on your first, second or third try

* Allow time to build and master your craft

* Keep researching about your business

* Stay Positive

* Keep negative thoughts to a minimum

* Replace every negative thought with 2 positive thoughts

* Be confident in anything you do even when you mess up

* Take the 1st step

* Practice what you preach – If you say you will get started on Monday, get started Sunday

* Ask your mentor for motivational material and videos

* Be Self-Disciplined

* Stick to your budget

* Discipline your disappointments

* Learn how to control your emotions

* Be Consistent

* Kill all excuses

Preface

This Entrepreneur success manual was designed to help you develop a strategy so you can apply them in your life for success and happiness. Catrina's primary mission is to help new entrepreneurs transition from the employee mindset. It will also help skilled entrepreneurs get to a new level of success. Find valuable information, resources, and tools needed to get on the right track.

When Catrina got into the field of helping others become entrepreneurs, she realized what was causing so many to fail. She saw how they would be so excited to become a boss, but lacked the knowledge and understanding of a boss. Many dream of earning money from the comfort of their own home while others start low-cost businesses to build their income. However, some don't realize the requirements needed to become successful.

The information provided was collected from Catrina's experiences, wisdom and knowledge within the last 10 years of being a successful internet entrepreneur, traditional business owner, professional speaker, and skilled network marketer. She is thankful for the inspiration she receives from family, supporters and business associates.

Use the white space in this book to write about your business ideas.

Winners never quit and quitters never win. – Vince Lombardi

Chapter 1. Introduction to Entrepreneurship

Week 1 Date:

An Entrepreneur is a person who organizes and manages their own time, money and life through business operations. It will require you to risk your time and finances. Your results will vary from the next person but most find working for themselves very rewarding. It is important to learn how to respect your process through the ups and downs. Successful entrepreneurs range from different ages, cultures and most of all their lifestyles. You can become a successful entrepreneur by creating a business plan and engaging in consistent action.

Working from home is a very challenging and rewarding way to earn income, however, it isn't for everyone. There are different categories in entrepreneurship. One category is the traditional businesses. A traditional business is where you have inventory, a building to run your daily operations and employees. Another category in entrepreneurship is an independent contractor. An independent contractor works on their own time, chooses their jobs, but may work for a company doing freelance work. There are many more categories in entrepreneurship.

Let's help you figure if becoming an entrepreneur is for you. Entrepreneurs are risk takers. You must have the right attitude and behavior to succeed at your business goals. It is when times seem hard when you must NOT Quit! You must be willing to turn your problems into possibilities.

Being an entrepreneur is not a get-rich-quick scheme. You must be committed, apply patience and motivation in the process. Setting goals, having a passion for something, and accepting that you will face trials and tribulations as a business owner will bring you one step closer to becoming a Successful Entrepreneur!

New & Skilled Entrepreneur Survey

Who do you currently listen to for success tips?
_____

Who is the first person you go to for advice? Why?
_____
_____

Would you trade lifestyles with the person you get advice from? _____

What type of business do you want to start?
_____

Why? _____

Note: Do not listen to negative people or those who haven't been where you want to go. Is it time to change who you listen to?

Why? _____

Preparation: New & Skilled Entrepreneurs

Preparation #1: Buy Notepad/Calendar/Pen within the next 7 days.

Preparation #2: Write down 1 new life goal each day for a total of 5 days. It can be life or business success goals.

Day 1 _____

Day 2 _____

Day 3 _____

Day 4 _____

Day 5 _____

Preparation: Entrepreneur Set-Up (Apply Self-Discipline)

Choose 3-4 days out of the week to start working your success manual.

Schedule 2-3 hours for each day. (Note: Do not over work yourself or you will get burnt out.)

Mon_____ Tues_____ Wed _____ Thurs_____ Fri_____
Sat_____ Sun_____

Name 3 things about you that is different from other people.

1) _____

2) _____

3) _____

What is your best learning method? It is important to know so that you can transform your mindset from an employee to an entrepreneur.

___ I learn best Hands On/Face-to-Face

___ I learn best Online/Webinars/Conference Calls

___ I am open to learning all ways

How much are you willing to sacrifice for your success? (Mark scale below between 1-10)

Scale

(1 - No work, no time) (5 - Put half time) (10- over achiever, hungry for success)

1 --------------------5--------------------10

You will complete different assessments throughout this manual to help you set a clear path towards your new world of success.

Chapter 2. Self-Assessments

Answer on a separate sheet so you can revisit in the future.

Week 2 Date:

(ABILITY)

* Write down 5 Strengths & 5 Weaknesses about yourself

* Be Honest (Ex. You may procrastinate on your top priorities.)

* Create 2 ways to turn those problems into Possibilities

(Example: {Problem} You are not a business owner but want to be one. {Possibility} Follow this manual consistently)

* Create 2 ways to go over and beyond your strengths (Example: Get business card for a more professional image)

* Define Critical Thinking and Reasoning

(INTEREST)

♥ What is one thing you love to do regardless if you get paid or not?

♥ Would you sacrifice time for you to succeed?

♥ Are you willing to pay others to help guide you to success?

♥ Are you willing to work on your business even when you get tired?

(MOTIVATION)

1. What is your true reason for getting up every day to earn money?

2. How will you apply critical thinking in your business?

3. How do you handle tough decisions?

4. Do you think before you act?

5. What type of multitasking do you think you will need to do in your business/profession?

6. What do you use for motivation?

7. How will you handle constructive criticism?

8. How will you handle stress and conflict with your customers, suppliers and employees in your business?

9. How can you WORK SMART, NOT HARD?

(PATIENCE)

♥ What would you do if things don't go as expected?

♥ Are you willing to wait up to a year to start receiving profits from your own business?

♥ Do you save money or let it burn your pocket the moment you get it?

Use these questions to give you a better understanding of your strengths and weaknesses. Strengthen your strengths and better your weaknesses. It also opens your mind for more ways to handle business challenges. There is not a right or wrong way to do business. It is important to evaluate your problems as they arise and use critical thinking for the best solution.

Chapter 3. Brainstorm

Week 3 Date:

Brainstorming is random thoughts about your interests, dream career, business, etc. It is important to think through different ideas when choosing to start your own business or a new career.

Think about things you have a passion for or even something you wouldn't mind doing for 5 hours or more a day. Catrina turned her good cleaning skills into a profitable business.

The key to brainstorming is having written notes. Write down all your ideas. Your friends and family may have some great ideas as well. Carry a small notebook with you when you are out and about because you never know when the answer you been looking for will come. It could come in the shower, on your way to work, in line at the grocery store, etc.

Brainstorm Activity

1. Rough Draft – Over the next 2 days, write down different business ideas. When something comes to mind, write it down, if someone says something that you may be interested in, write it down. This is what brainstorming entails.

2. Think about things you would love to do all the time. Write down a minimum of 10 ideas. If you feel stuck, ask Google for business ideas. Now look at each idea and evaluate them. Can you see yourself doing the necessary actions that business idea requires for a minimum 5 years? Choose your top 2 business ideas. Your next step is to start your research to see which one you could realistically start.

1. Research Process

Separate Sheet – Draw 5 rows (left to right) Leave 3-4 lines to write in per column. Put the type of business at the top of the page. Name each row listed below.

a. Business Items Needed

b. Competition Name

c. Market Trends – Supply & Demand – What do people want?

d. Sales & Promotions – How will you attract your customers? Think of 3 creative ways that could attract your customers.

3. Personal Survey – Ask 5 questions you can ask the ones closest to you. Post them on Facebook for your friends, family and people who know you to respond. Call your co-workers, friends and family and get 3-5 answers per question. Write each response.

a. Do you believe I can succeed as a business owner or stick to my career?

b. What kind of special talents and skills do you see in me?

c. Am I organized or unorganized?

d. Do I budget my money or let money burn my pockets?

e. What do you see as a priority in my life?

The purpose of this survey is for your co-workers, friends and family to evaluate you. Do not take it personal. You must be able to accept criticism in the business world. It is up to you to let it make you or break you. Knowing how people view you will allow you to strengthen your weaknesses.

4. Business Survey – write 3 business oriented questions about your type of business. (Example – Cleaning Business: Do you ever have enough time to clean your entire home?)

5. Description of Business/Success you have. Ask others what do they think about you going into this field of work?

Note: Be careful who you ask. If you ask a person who is always negative, you may get a negative answer.

Entrepreneur Questionnaire

Answer these next set of questions truthfully. This is to see where you stand.

1. Are you fit to be an Entrepreneur?? Take an entrepreneur survey.

https://www.surveymonkey.com/r/7XNHLYY

2. Why do you want to be a successful entrepreneur?

_____

3. How long have you been thinking about starting a business?

_____

4. What is your definition of success?

_____
_____

5. How long have you worked for others?
_____

6. Are you willing to search for the best solution?
_____

7. How much time are you willing to put in for your business?
_____

8. Are you willing to make ethical business decisions?
_____

9. How are you going to stay up-to-date with your business and competition?
_____

10. How much are you willing to invest in yourself?
_____

11. How often are you willing to update yourself, clients and suppliers about your business status?
_____

Chapter 4 Planning Phase

Week 4 Date: _____

The planning phase requires putting to-do tasks in place with set dates. The building blocks in planning help determine what job tasks is needed and how to carry out the plan. Be prepared to work out your goals.

You will divide your planning phase into two main parts. One part will be short term goals. These are goals for today, tomorrow and within the current year. The second part will be long term goals. Long term goals are plans longer than one year. It requires you to create dreams. Dreams are something big you want to go for. If you are not dreaming, you are dying.

Categorize your short and long-term goals. These categories are finances, personal development, and a list of things you want. Review your goals daily.

1. Document all the tasks required to do business.

a. Create 3-5 short-term goals – Example: Set business start-up date for less than 1 year

b. Create 3-5 long-term goals

i. Break down your long-term goals into smaller/short-term goals to keep you motivated and prioritize each one

c. Set realistic goals

2. Will you need other people to help you carry out your task? (example: logo designers for your business cards, etc.)

a. Buy business cards – short or long-term goal

b. Website designer – short or long-term goal

c. Buy Business License (if required) – short term goal

d. Suppliers for your product or service

3. How much money will it take to start your company?

a. Inventory costs

b. Office supplies

c. Customer Relations tools – Business expense software

4. How much time will you need to carry out your plan?

5. Plan leisure and family time – Discuss your goals with your family and significant other. Come to an agreement on expectations from each other.

6. Plan to add more goals and completion dates over time.

Mark goals off as you complete them. Planning your goals may not be completed at the perfect time or place. It is up to you to recognize the progress, evaluate the results and make changes where necessary. Don't forget to celebrate your achievements.

Prepare to build your clientele/customers.

Write 100 names & numbers (Use Memory Jogger- Google)

* Add 15 Names and #'s List - per day -Ongoing process

**** Schedule a pre-launch call/meet-up to your friends and family to share your exciting news.

They may not be able to attend your 1st, 2nd or 3rd invitation to learn more about your business. Take control of your emotions and plan to follow up later in the future.

Invitation Process: Make your call than 60 seconds. Have excitement in your voice. Invite 20-30 people minimum.

First Step

Example Script: Hello, is this Kim? Hey Kim, this is Catrina. How are you doing? I don't want to take too much of your time, do you have 30 seconds? I'm so excited because I'm launching my new business and I want to celebrate with my friends and family. What are you doing on (Date)? I'd like to invite you as a V.I.P. guest to join me. Can I count on your support?

Second Step

Have a professional friend or family to call and remind everyone 1 day before your launch day.

Third Step

This time you call on the day of your launch and make sure they have the address and right time? Inform them you will have something for them. Ask can they bring something less than $3 to your event? (Ice, Soda, etc.)

Get an updated script based on the type of business you are in. It is important to invite 20-30 people because everyone may not make it on your launch date. Things happen and not anyone is perfect. Be prepared to have another call/event to share your business.

Time Management

Time management will be an important aspect of your journey. It's what you do with your time that determines your results. Update your planner/calendar daily. On a separate sheet of paper, fill out your schedule based on the number of hours provided below. Filling in the time slot and to-do tasks will help you gain a consistent routine. The hourly breakdown was inspired from the book, *The Magic of Thinking Big* by David Schwartz. It may take 14-21 days to get the hang of it. Have patience as you learn a new way to manage your time.

There are 168 hours per week.

51 hours – Work - Based on average 40 hours work per week

50 hours – Sleep/Rest – Based on average 8 hours per day

25 hours – Eating- Based on 2-3 hours per day preparing/cooking and eating dinner

14 hours – Free Time – Up to 2 hours of fun, reading, playing around w/ loved ones

18 hours – Up to 2.5 hours per day to work on your business

10 hours – Up to 1 free time per day

Positive results will follow if you manage your time.

* Productive work day

* Achieve more goals

* Quality work

* Less stress

* Great reputation with clients

Negative consequences will follow if you fail to manage your time.

* Rushed work

* Half done work

* Poor work quality

* Added stress

* Bad reputation with clients

There are two types of leaders in the world. Which one are you? Check one

___First type of leader is a go getter. They do what they can without someone telling them. They are willing to go over and beyond for their success. They make no excuses, and get it done.

___Second type of leader is already comfortable in life. They only do what is told, but they still do the minimum. They don't even try to go over & beyond. Always have an excuse to justify why they can't. Neither have integrity to do what they say they will do.

Chapter 5. Research & Notate

Week 5 Date: _____

Day 1 Business Brainstorm Idea 1
_____

Day 3 Business Brainstorm Idea 2
_____

Day 5 Business Brainstorm Idea 3
_____

Think of a business name. Write down different names until you find the one you like. Make it catchy, easy to spell and stand out. Use another sheet of paper to think of more.

_____

_____

_____

Research Your Business:

Write down everything you know about the business.

1. Why do customers buy your type of products or services?

2. How much is the average Salary/Pay for your business?

3. Market Demand – Who are your customers? What type of products or services do they buy?

* Responsibilities of job. What is required from you?

* Who is your Competition?

* Research Competition On/Offline

* Check pricing

* Services Offered

* Service Locations

* Customer/Employee Policy

* Demand in your city for business

* Check Demographics – Average Income

* Tools/supplies/items needed for business

* Search for best equipment

* Best way to provide service/product

* Owner equity/money needed to start business

* Legal

* Business License Requirement – Areas – Contact City Hall

* Price for license, additional fees, expiry dates

* Retail/liquor/Revenue taxes?

* IRS EIN (Get one free at IRS.gov)

* Employee/Business Partner Info

* Bank Details (Traditional Business)

* Insurance, Bond info (Traditional Business)

Education

* Read 3 self-development books that would benefit you and your business

* Start-up business advice

* Related to your career field, business, or industry

* Continued education within your business is critical - Is it required frequently?

* Motivation and Inspiration that will keep you going

Personal Development

* Take a personality test- Learn new characteristics about yourself. https://www.16personalities.com/free-personality-test

* Find a mentor who already achieved the success milestone in your business field.

Chapter 6. Financial Management

Week 6 Date:_____

Start preparing for your business. Expect to go through trials and tribulations as you launch your business. Preparing your business plan will avoid massive business failure in the long run.

90 Day Income Goals _____ **Date:**

_____

New Financial Goal: Save $5 per week for business. Check the box if you accomplished your money-saving goal

Week # 1 Saved $5 ☐ Date _____

Week # 2 Saved $5 ☐ Date _____

Week # 3 Saved $5 ☐ Date _____

Week # 4 Saved $5 ☐ Date _____

Financial Plan (Budget)

Add your total income per month. Add your total expenses. Add your total needs (personal, business needs).

* Gross Income/Loss

* Expenses

* Needs

* Wants

You need to understand where your money is going on a daily, weekly, and monthly basis. This will allow you to cut out unnecessary spending that could go toward your business.

For example: you may spend extra (free) money on clothes, junk food, etc. That money could be saved toward your new business. Don't let money burn your pocket on materialistic things.

How long will it take to start up? How much money is needed? What would you need to become legal? (Business License, Certifications, etc.)

Budget your Money

Example

Income	2017	Jan	Feb	Mar	April	May	June	Total
Job Name								0
Business Name								0

Expenses	Miles	Food	Gas	Car Bills	House Bills	Total
January		0	0	0	0	0
Feb						0
Mar						0
April						0
May						0
June						0
July						0
August						0
Sept						0
Oct						0
Nov						0
Dec						0
Total	0	0	0	0	0	0

Chapter 7. Business Plan

Week 7 Date: _____

Create a Business Plan

This is an important task to create when going into business. A business plan will help guide you to accomplish your business dreams and goals. There are many business resources that will help you create a business plan.

Your business plan is what will determine your success rate. This is the time you should choose which business entity is best for your business. (Sole Proprietorship, LLC, Corporation)

Important factors to put into your business plan includes:

Business Plan: Executive Summary

This summary gives a brief description of the type of service, service location, market targets and projected growth within 5 years of your business. Add your objectives and company mission in this section.

Objectives are basic tools and goals you plan to utilize to achieve your business goals. Be sure to list the objectives of your company for the first 3 years of operation. Your mission should be a statement describing the purpose of your company or organization. It should express the primary actions of the company.

* Company Summary

This should describe your company in detail. What type of ownership will you have? Describe the history of your company. How long you have been in business. Where is the location of your business? Include your legal establishment of the company. What are your start-up plans?

* Product or Service

Describe in detail what you are selling. Focus on the advantages for the customer. Do a competition comparison. Will you use any technology? Include any future products or services.

* Market Analysis Summary

Describe your market, customer needs, where they are, and how you will reach them. Have a backup plan in this summary.

* Strategy and Implementation Summary

Be specific. Include management responsibilities with dates and budgets. Make sure you can track results.

* Management Summary

Describe the organization structure and the key management team members. What are your goals for the management to help the business succeed?

* Financial Plan

How will you survive in your business after you have made income and accrued expenses? Make sure to include at the very least your projected profit and loss and Cash Flow tables. Include things such as key financial indicators, break-even analysis, projected cash flow, projected balance sheet and long-term plans. Research each term that you don't understand.

Customer Service

Customer service is key to success throughout your business life. Customers are always first in business. Make goals to build confidence and bonds with each client. As your business grows, ask clients and employees to have patience with you. That is a part of the communication process with customers so they don't lose confidence in your company. The reason you ask for patience is because as you expand you will have growing pains. Have patience with your customers and put yourself in their shoes just as you ask for patience from them. Remember customer service is key to success!

Chapter 8. Marketing Plan

Week 8 Date: _____

Create a Marketing Plan

A marketing plan is vital to the success of your business. This plan will describe how you will market your business, strengths and weaknesses, competition, pricing and more. Visit the link for an outline http://www.quickmba.com/marketing/plan/.

Ask 20 people that know you the following questions below. (Keep track of your responses for future reference.)

Question #1: Would you prefer to support a small business owner or big corporation?

Question #2: How would you want a company to show you appreciation?

Question #3: What type of things will make you want to be a repeat customer?

Ask friends, family, & social media friends what would it take to win them as customers. Write down your top responses.

* _____

* _____

* _____

* _____

* Understand Time Management - Planning activities effectively in time blocks for production.

* What you do with your time reflects how you will succeed.

* Pay attention to what is needed right now rather than doing things right, so that success will grow in the future.

* Understand Marketing your business - Strategies to get your product/service in front of customers.

* Understand Managing your business - What are your day to day operations?

* Understand success in business - Whatever you create as goals is your success. Do not compare others success to yours because everyone has different dreams and goals.

* Understand how to be organized - To put together into an orderly fashion where everything is functioning as a structured whole.

* Sometimes your to-do list can grow to the point where it gets out of control. Some key steps to avoid being unorganized is to:

* Break big tasks down into smaller ones

* Monitor how your energy & time is spent

* Ask yourself "what is the best use of your time right now?"

* Start and End each work session with 10 minutes of straightening up.

* Network with others (Potential clients, investors, helpers)

Networking

Networking will help expand every aspect of your business.

Start by creating a profile on social networking sites. You will see enhanced clientele and increase profits as you increase your marketing budget. Start small if your funds are limited.

Online Networks

* Facebook (Create a separate business page through your personal page)

* Twitter

* Instagram

* Merchant Circle

* LinkedIn

* Craigslist

* Meetup

Offline Networks

* Word of Mouth

* Newspaper

* Mailing Ads

* Advertise in Magazines

* Rent Event Booths

Blog

Blog about your business because that will bring more traffic to your business website.

Are you prepared for failure/success?

1. What other type of income will you have coming in during your first 2 years of business?

2. How long do you plan to run your business alone?

3. What is the plan b if the first business doesn't work out?

4. Do you have realistic goals? How do you know? Ask around?

5. Would it be best to upgrade to better systems or software soon?

6. How focused are you on each task?

7. Do you have set Priorities? Do you know that they can change? What will you do if they do change?

Chapter 9. Business Resources

Week 9 Date: _____

Research free business resources/assistance for success in your business. It is best to take advantage of all your free business tools first. There are seminars and free business coaching that will help you with preparing a business plan. **(Contact CatrinaLatriceWilliams.com to help connect you with your local area business resources.)**

* Business Seminars (list for them to access) –Join these seminars that can help you build clientele for your business. http://www.charlestonbusiness.com/community/calendar

* Score Counselor – Retired business owners that will help you with business resources and guidance for your business. http://www.score.com

* Minority business support - http://www.charleston-sc.gov/dept/content.aspx?nid=2082

* State business resources – Trident One Stop - http://www.toscc.org/

* Small business administration – http://www.sba.gov

* Small business seminars/resources – search Google for your local area

Tax Information

Entrepreneurs are considered self-employed when filing their tax returns with the IRS. Once you make $400 within one year, it is important to get a business license with your local town hall. However, it depends on the type of business you start. You are required to pay income tax and self-employment tax (SE tax) which include Social Security and Medicare tax.

There are many great benefits to self-employment. You can write off business expenses to deduct from your income. Schedule C or Schedule C-EZ is used to report your income and expenses from your business. Some expenses are business supplies, home office supplies, rent or mortgage, utilities, marketing expenses just to name a few.

Decide what form of business entity to establish before you open your business. Most entrepreneurs start off as a Sole Proprietor and move up from there. The IRS recommend you choose your tax preparer wisely. Visit the IRS website for more information https://www.irs.gov/individuals/self-employed#structures.

Grant & Government Contract

Most grants are given to non-profit organizations. Find out more at Http://www.Grants.Gov. On the other hand, you can apply for government contracts for your business. Apply for a D-U-N-S Number (FREE) to start bidding on government contracts. Learn more here: https://www.sba.gov/contracting/getting-started-contractor/get-d-u-n-s-number

Chapter 10. Action Steps

Week 10 Date:_____

Congratulations! You have officially started steps to transition your mind from an employee to an entrepreneur. Now it's time to act by implementing your business and marketing plan. Do not fade away from this manual since you have completed it.

* Create a Progress tracking form

* Review this e-book regularly and update your business results accordingly.

* Be sure to review your manual on a weekly basis until the information become second nature!

* Advanced Saving Plan– Save $10 up to $200 per month/week for the rest of the year.

Reality Check

Do not expect to get-rich-quick. Successful business owners put in time.

Now turn your dreams into reality.

When do you Quit your Day Job?

Once you have researched and planned your business, the next step is to prepare to finance your business. Expect to keep working your day job for a minimum of 18 months before expecting to see great profits from your business. From there is when you can plan when to quit your day job.

This is for informational purposes only. Results vary per person. If you found this helpful, please tag Catrina Latrice Williams on

[Facebook](#) to share your review or visit www.CatrinaLatriceWilliams.com. Pre-Order her next book, *Fail your way to Success*.

Important Info.

Results may vary based on the industry, individual motivation, planning, decision making and dedication.

Dream Board Project

Completing your dream board will help you have a clearer vision of success. It's only right to vision your dreams and goals now that you have your guide to success. A dream board is very easy to create. Start collecting different magazines that have things you put as your short and long-term goals. Look at Catrina's dream board she made in 2014 as an example. She has seen many of her dreams come true. There is no right or wrong way. Now it's your turn to turn your dreams into reality.

Items Needed

Poster Board

Magazines

Scissors

Glue

New Entrepreneur Money Tips

Earning money from home requires entrepreneur knowledge along with self-determination. Most jobs from home will consider you to be an independent contractor. As an independent contractor, you can write off business expenses. Things such as paying your electric bill would be a business expense when you work from home. It is important to keep track, and organize of the main business categories such as supplies, food, vehicle mileage, and more. Self-employed see great tax benefits compared to regular W2 employees. It is important to categorize and organize business expenses monthly.

There are legit ways to earn money from home. Catrina has been testing work from home jobs over the last 10 years. She would apply, invest as necessary and put in consistent action to see if everything was legit about the companies. She had her lawyer to research multiple companies to assure their legitimacy. She has earned thousands of dollars working primarily from home in companies such as data entry, call center jobs, network marketing and much more.

It is important to treat your work at home job like you are working a regular job. If you don't put in any activity or production then there is not any income generated to look forward to. There are legit ways to earn a full-time income from home. You can find opportunities like that on Catrina's website.

Her website provides details on free work from home opportunities to lucrative businesses that entails giving an investment.

You must be willing to allow a mentor to guide you with the work at home job you choose. Sign up for Catrina's Money Workshop.

How much can I get paid?

The pay from home is determined by the job you choose. Certain jobs that allow you to do data entry will pay up to a dollar per task. Multiple tasks completed properly in one day can lead to ones, tens, hundreds and thousands of dollars. Call center jobs starting pay normally start at $8 and up per hour. There are freelance jobs and more that will pay up to $25 per hour based on restrictions.

Start your $1000 Journey with Multiple Sources from Home (Example Time & Money Schedule)

- **Primary Home Job**

    - Call Center Job - Pay $10/hour - Work 5 hours

    - 4 days per week $200 * 4 weeks = $800 Month

    Part Time Side Jobs

- Surveys/Opinions $3 per day 1 hour - 20 days = $60 per month
- Transcribe - $1 per day (1-2 hours)- 20 days = $20 per month
- Data Entry- pay varies - up to $10 per job (1-2 hours)- $40 per month
- Write Articles - up to $5-10 per day 1-2 hrs. per day - 5 days - $80-160 per month
- Travel Agent - Booking Cruises – 75% Commission (Ex. 10 person cruise - $600) 60-90 day payouts

    Choose your jobs based on skills, interest

    Visit CatrinaLatriceWilliams.com to get started earning money from home.

www.ingramcontent.com/pod-product-compliance
Lightning Source LLC
Chambersburg PA
CBHW050028230526
45470CB00003B/1185